An Artist's America

BY Michael Albert

Henry Holt

AND COMPANY

New York

This book is dedicated to
MY COUNTRY, the United States of America;
MY PARENTS, Larry and Wendy Albert;
MY BROTHERS, David and Douglas;
MY WIFE AND BEST FRIEND, Erynn;
OUR CHILDREN, Lucy, Mary, John, and Jane; and
AMERICA'S CHILDREN (of all ages),
who I hope will be inspired to create
and follow their own ideas of
THE AMERICAN DREAM.

I would also like to thank my friend
John Fernandez whose support
and encouragement are immeasurable.

Henry Holt and Company, LLC
Publishers since 1866
175 Fifth Avenue
New York, New York 10010
www.HenryHoltKids.com

Henry Holt® is a registered trademark of Henry Holt and Company, LLC.
Copyright © 2008 by Michael Albert
All rights reserved.
Distributed in Canada by H. B. Fenn and Company Ltd.

Library of Congress Cataloging-in-Publication Data
Albert, Michael.
An artist's America / Michael Albert.—1st ed.
    p.   cm.
ISBN-13: 978-0-8050-7857-2
ISBN-10: 0-8050-7857-6
1. United States—Civilization—Pictorial works—Juvenile literature.
2. Popular culture—United States—Pictorial works—Juvenile literature.
3. United States—History—Pictorial works—Juvenile literature.
4. United States—In art—Juvenile literature. I. Title.
E169.1.A4675 2008   709.2—dc22   2007006978

First Edition—2008 / Designed by Elynn Cohen
Printed in China on acid-free paper. ∞

1 3 5 7 9 10 8 6 4 2

CONTENTS

EPIC WORKS

RESOURCES

INTRODUCTION

In the beginning, I started drawing— I would draw on anything (even an air sickness bag!).

First, I doodled with pen and ink, number 2 pencils, colored pencils, Magic Markers, crayons, and eventually experimented with wax oil crayons. This was while I was still in college, studying business at New York University. I visited museums, such as the Metropolitan Museum of Art and the Museum of Modern Art, and looked at art that inspired me. At the time, I particularly loved the work of van Gogh, Matisse, Cézanne, Monet, Vuillard, Gauguin, Klimt, Modigliani, Seurat, and Picasso. There were many excellent examples of these artists' work in New York City's museums.

New York City (e)scape

The Victim

THE VICTIM

I attempted to make art in my own style. This drawing is actually a montage of all the brands and other personal items found in my dorm room. I put myself in the foreground of the drawing (as Henri Matisse did in some of his sketches) and called it *The Victim* because I felt like I was the victim of advertising and marketing. Many of the collages I've made over the years have a similar look and feel to this early wax oil crayon drawing.

THE FACES

The Faces series began as simple doodles in pen, pencil, marker, and many combinations therein. I enjoy drawing portraits—prefacing that the only thing I am sure of is that the drawing will NOT look identical to the person! My faces often turned out expressive and revealing of human emotion in an abstract sense. I soon began creating full-color compositions of this theme. I also started to title many of my pieces. A good title can make a work of art even more interesting.

The Pain of the Weight of the World

SIR REAL

Sir Real is an art concept and series of cartoon-like characters that parody the modern art movement of Surrealism. I created this series when I realized the necessity and value of developing my own merchandising brand for my Natural Foods distribution business. Today I make and sell organic fruit juices that feature these characters on the bottle labels. The Red Apple Man is on the label of organic apple cider; the Lemon Man and the Tangerine Man are on the labels of lemonade and tangerine juices. These characters wear bowler hats and tuxedoes because of the brand's motto: "Life is a formal occasion."

The Sir Real slogan is "Eye Have a Dream" (or, in other words, "Do what you love") and its creed is "Do the Ripe Thing," which is what I try to do (the "right thing," that is), in both my personal and my professional life. These are ideas that I believe are worth thinking about and promoting.

Sir Real Red Apple Man

Sir Real Lemon Man

Sir Real Tangerine Man

Sir Real juices on
store shelves

THE EMPIRE STATE BUILDING

I created collages as a way to recycle certain paper products I had accumulated at work and home. I had been making mostly drawings and started to experiment with new materials.

First, I began using stickers, photographs, and old labels from my juice business (cutting them into pieces and arranging them on cardboard). I started making photo-collage portraits of family and friends, then other subjects.

This collage of the Empire State Building was made from a postcard that I cut into strips, rectangular slivers, and then rearranged to form my own composition. It is a Cubist portrait of one of the world's most famous buildings. I created this artwork for an exhibition I had on the ground level of the Empire State Building. I thought it was a terrific venue for Pop Art, being a major tourist attraction in New York City.

The Empire State Building

Flag

THE FLAG

The flag is a classic theme in Pop Art, made famous in the 1950s by Jasper Johns. My flags are also inspired by Betsy Ross, whose hand-sewn flags were made from cut pieces of colored cloth. My first flag collages were created from United States Postal Service Priority Mail stickers that I cut and pasted onto pieces of cardboard. Later, after I had been working with cereal boxes and other consumer packaging, I started making flags out of the red, white, and blue packaging. In all, I have created over three hundred renditions of this classic American theme.

In this particular *Flag*, the red pieces came from a Coca-Cola twelve-pack carton and the blue pieces came from a Frosted Flakes cereal box.

CEREALISM AND THE POP CUBIST PORTRAITS

FROSTED FLAKES
Portrait of an American Classic

I began using consumer packaging such as cereal, cookie, and tea boxes. After I created an abstract cereal box collage out of a Frosted Flakes box, I made a series of Pop Cubist portraits of popular consumer brands. I called the cereal box collages Cerealism, and also created portraits of other classic American brands and iconic images.

I deconstructed the cover by cutting it into many small pieces and then reconstructed it. After mixing up the elements, I found it fascinating that the original image was almost instantly recognizable.

This is the first collage I made using a cereal box cover. I have created over five hundred original pieces of art in the Cerealism series.

Frosted Flakes #1 (Portrait of an American Classic)

Cheerios on Black (Random Angles)

CHEERIOS

This is the only product I can think of that babies eat as their first food and adults continue eating through-out their lives. The Cheerios box is also one of the most familiar icons in the supermarket brandscape. No matter how I reconstructed the box cover, it was obviously Cheerios.

Cheerios (Boardwalk Effect)

TRIX

After creating my first group of individual cereal box collages, I decided to take three or four of the same box and make Master Cerealist Portraits in a larger format. This *Trix* portrait is one in this series.

CAP'N CRUNCH BERRIES

As I developed the Cerealism series, I started experimenting with a variety of shapes, such as the swirl in this Cap'n Crunch collage.

Trix (Master Cerealist Portrait)

1999

Cap'n Crunch Berries

CRACKER JACK

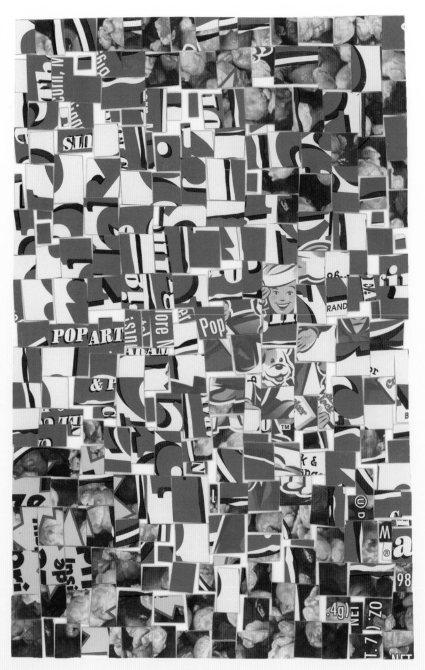

Cracker Jack

Besides cereal boxes, I also tried to capture many other classic brands. *Cracker Jack*, featuring a snack food offered at baseball games, is one of my sports-related works. I made this from an actual Cracker Jack box, which is hard to find now that the box has been replaced by a printed cellophane bag.

CAMPBELL'S SOUP

Many people have described my work as a cross between Andy Warhol's Pop Art and Cubism. So, in honor of Warhol and his most well-known subject, here is my portrait of the Campbell's Soup can label.

Campbell's Soup

Federal Reserve Note (Portrait of Washington)

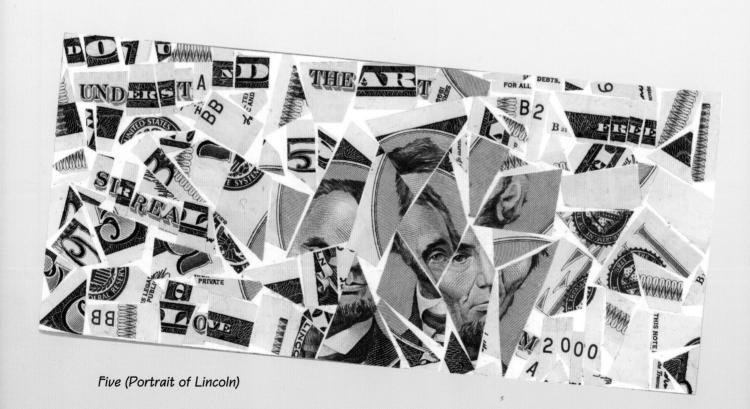

Five (Portrait of Lincoln)

PORTRAITS OF WASHINGTON AND LINCOLN

Federal Reserve Note and Five

Currency is perhaps the most well-known series of images in our world. No matter how much I dissect its visual elements, it remains recognizable.

I'm constantly asked if it's legal to make art from money. I thought this was a good example of the absurd situations we are often in. We can ruin our paper money accidentally running it through the wash, but when we take the same bill and make art out of it, people question our intent. Then again, I wouldn't recommend cutting up too much of your money!

EPIC WORKS

Over time, I started using entire boxes (not just the front panels) to make my collages, and combined elements of many different boxes to create larger-scale, more complex compositions. Sometimes I collected characters from many different brands; at other times, logos, and then letters and words. Some works combined all these elements.

THE LAST BREAKFAST

The epic works are my largest and most detailed collages. They are epic in both subject matter and the amount of work it takes to make them, usually months. I've re-created numerous episodes from the Bible and American history. What I especially love about being an artist is getting the chance to pick subjects I am interested in, learning about them at my own pace, and then expressing what I've learned through art.

I started depicting famous biblical and historical events, including the Last Supper (my version being *The Last Breakfast*), Judgment Day, Lincoln's Gettysburg Address, the Statue of Liberty, the Pledge of Allegiance, and the signing of the Declaration of Independence.

The Last Breakfast

Judgement Day

JUDGEMENT* DAY

Of all the artworks I've created, *Judgement* Day* took the longest. I worked on this collage for an entire year. Since no one escapes the final judgment, I felt every possible character I could find must be included. I obsessively searched for hundreds of different characters from the packages of consumer brands. I put my Sir Real characters in the foreground as the panel of judges and included forty-nine words throughout the composition, which I thought one might consider at the time of judgment.

*actual spelling of original artwork

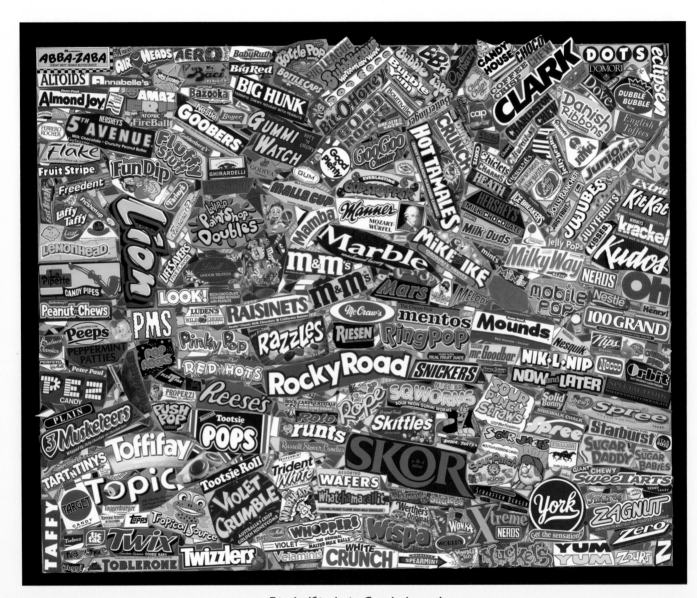

Etude (Study in Candy Logos)

ETUDE

Study in Candy Logos, A to Z

Etude is a study of logos of well-known candy brands. I chose to feature the candy in alphabetical order after making a collage with no particular order. That one drove me crazy because for every logo I wanted to add to the composition I found myself having to look at every piece that was already included to make sure I wasn't replicating it. I think this piece illustrates the incredible variety of choices we have in America. *Etude* was the centerpiece of an exhibition at Dylan's Candy Bar in New York City.

YOU KNOW WHAT THEY SAY

This composition is actually a collection of proverbs or clichés—words of wisdom that we hear all the time in our daily lives. This is the most highly detailed collage I've created to date.

You Know What They Say

THE GETTYSBURG ADDRESS

I was attracted to this subject simply because it is one of the most-famous speeches in American history. The creation of this work and the sharing of it with others encouraged my own in-depth study of the life of Lincoln and the Civil War. During the making of this piece, I memorized the address and often enjoy reciting it for others as they read along with the collage.

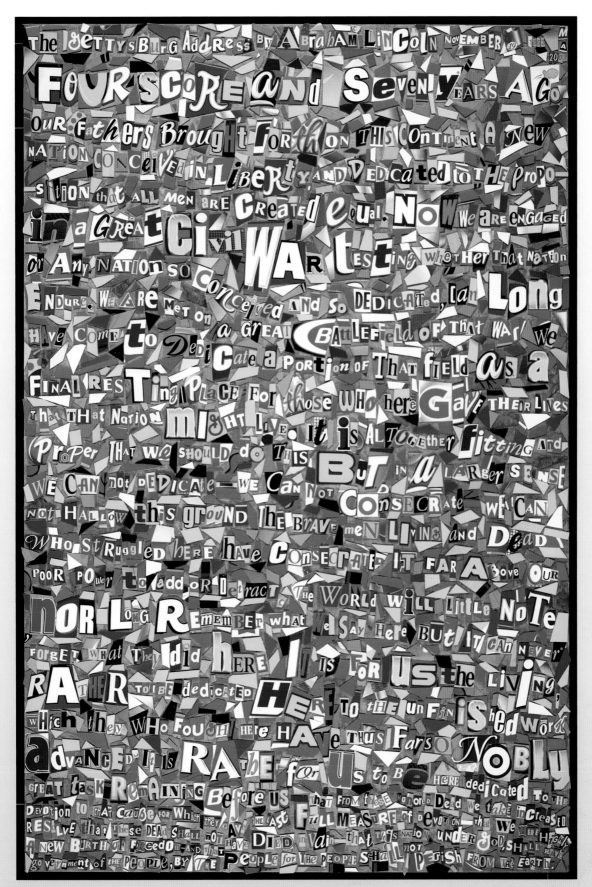

The Gettysburg Address

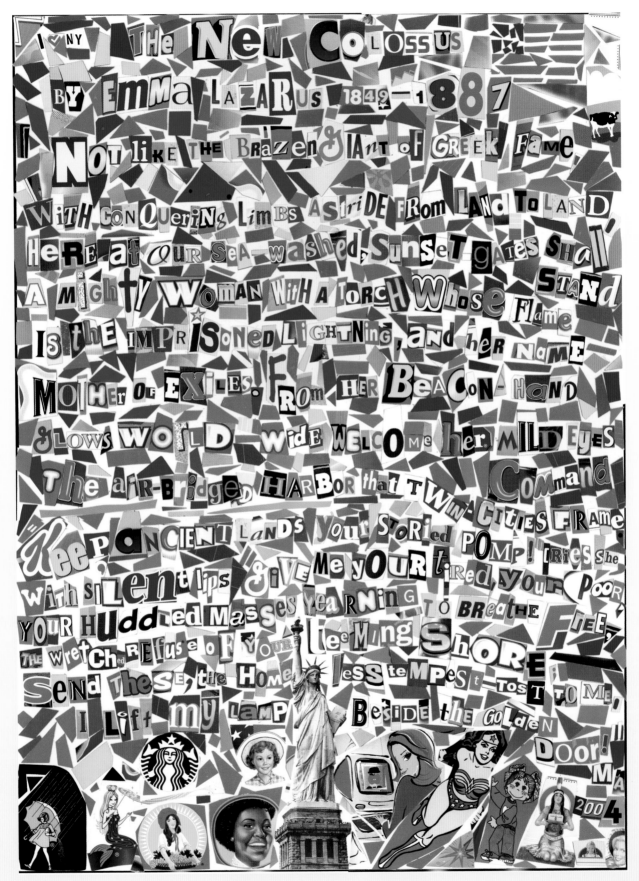

The Statue of Liberty ("The New Colossus")

THE STATUE OF LIBERTY

"The New Colossus" by Emma Lazarus

This is my interpretation of the fourteen-line poem, written by Emma Lazarus, that appears on the base of the Statue of Liberty. I found that most people (including myself) generally only know "Give me your tired, your poor, / Your huddled masses...."

I often refer to this collage as my "girl power" piece with Lady Liberty as the central figure surrounded by her twelve female apostles. Inspired by the film *The Wizard of Oz*, I created Lady Liberty in black and white (like Kansas), while everything else is in full color (like the Land of Oz), representing our Technicolor world of consumerism.

MOUNT RUSHMORE

Blue pieces cut from a Rice Krispies box depict the sky. There's a line from "The Star-Spangled Banner" embedded in the center. I chose these classic icons of pop-consumer culture—Mr. Clean, the Quaker Oats man, Cap'n Crunch, and Colonel Sanders—to represent the four presidents depicted on Mount Rushmore—Washington, Jefferson, Theodore Roosevelt, and Lincoln—because they shared similar features.

Mount Rushmore

The Pledge of Allegiance

THE PLEDGE
OF ALLEGIANCE

Before leading a collage work-shop for kindergarteners, I wanted a subject kids could easily recite. The Pledge of Allegiance seemed the perfect choice. I went back to my studio and spent more than a month creating this collage using images from hundreds of different sources. I picked fifty brand icons to represent the fifty states and used as many widely recognizable brand typefaces as I could find for the letters.

THE NUMBER PI
The First 190 Digits

After talking with a graduate student in mathematics about the number pi, I grew eager to create a mathematical collage. I saved numbers from packaging until I had a pile for my pi compositions. I looked up the first 10,000 digits of pi and taped it on the wall of my studio. I have done several versions of *Pi* going out as far as 277 digits, but this one also features seven words hinting at abstract ideas hidden within the patterns of numbers.

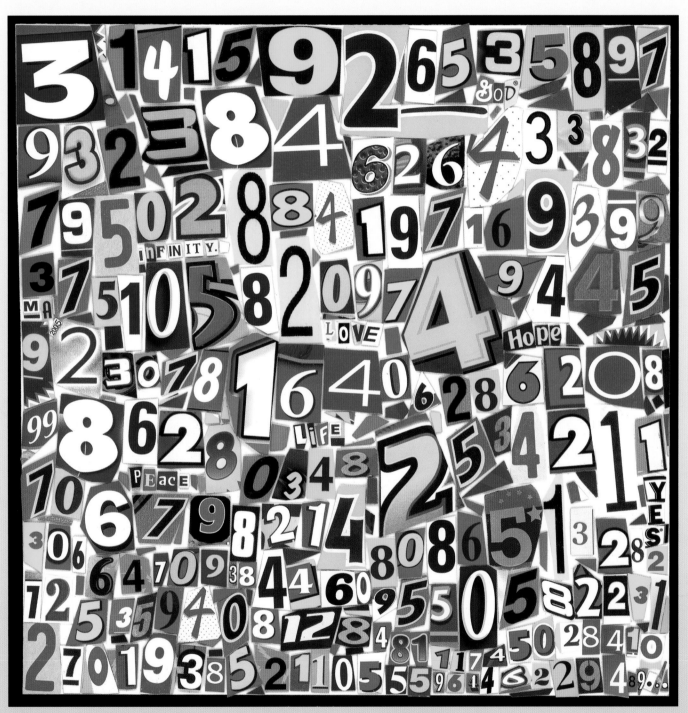

The Number Pi (The First 190 Digits)

The Signing of the Declaration of Independence

THE SIGNING OF THE DECLARATION OF INDEPENDENCE

This epic work is the culmination of over six months of research. I was especially drawn to the document's poetic nature and historic significance. I picked key portions of the text to lead the viewer on a journey, and selected fifty-six characters from our modern consumer world to represent the fifty-six statesmen who signed it. I also chose thirteen classic brands to represent the original thirteen colonies. The initials of all fifty-six statesmen are hidden in the composition. Samuel Adams, the statesman and brewer of beer, is the only character who was present at the actual signing.

WORKSHOPS

ot too long after I started to publicly show my work in museums, galleries, and nontraditional venues, I began getting calls from teachers and parents asking if I would come to their schools and give workshops on collage-making.

Over the years, I've led many workshops and have found that people of all ages enjoy creating collages. These workshops shed light on the deeper issue of consumer waste.

Kids are empowered to recycle through art, the materials needed are abundant and free (as opposed to painting supplies, for example, which are very expensive). The characters and typefaces associated with these packages make up a modern hieroglyphics that we see all the time, but they take on a whole new meaning when rearranged.

Today I continue to create new collages and give workshops to help foster an appreciation for art and a new generation of awareness regarding recycling issues. Through my art, I hope I can inspire others to do what they love and to express themselves in the process.

HOW TO MAKE COLLAGES
IN MY STYLE

To make collages from consumer packaging, you will need:

1 **Cardboard packaging** of a consumer brand, such as a cereal box, tea box, or cookie package.

2 **Glue stick**, preferably clear paper glue with a sponge valve-controlled applicator.

3 **Scissors**. Most scissors can cut cardboard consumer packaging. Younger kids may need help cutting the boxes, but they can also tear them, which adds a texture to collages.

4 **Cardboard for collage surface**. I often conduct workshops where the cardboard we work on is cut from the back of the box or some section of the box to make the artwork completely recycled, which is my concept in its purest sense.

5 **Workspace**. You don't need a lot of space, any table will do, but use newspaper under your work, or some other protection for the surface.

6 **Time**. The amount of time and effort that goes into your work will surely be evident in the result.

7 **A pen to sign and date your work.** It's a great way to keep track of your progress. It also shows that you take your work seriously.

ART CREDITS

Campbell's Soup (1998), 5" x 7$\frac{1}{8}$" collage of soup can label on hand-cut museum board. Collection of the artist.

Cap'n Crunch Berries (1998), 7$\frac{1}{2}$" x 10$\frac{1}{4}$" cereal box collage on hand-cut museum board. Collection of the artist.

Cheerios (Boardwalk Effect) (1998), 7$\frac{3}{8}$" x 10$\frac{3}{4}$" cereal box collage on hand-cut black museum board. Collection of the artist.

Cheerios on Black (Random Angles) (1997), 7$\frac{3}{8}$" x 10$\frac{5}{8}$" cereal box collage on hand-cut black museum board. Collection of the artist.

Cracker Jack (1999), 6$\frac{1}{4}$" x 10" collage on hand-cut museum board. Collection of the artist.

The Empire State Building (2000), 4$\frac{1}{8}$" x 6$\frac{1}{5}$" postcard collage on board. Private collection.

Etude (Study in Candy Logos, A to Z) (2002), 40" x 32" collage composition on acid-free cardboard. Private collection: Englewood, New Jersey.

Federal Reserve Note (Portrait of Washington) (1997), 6$\frac{1}{8}$" x 2$\frac{3}{4}$" collage of U.S. currency cut and pasted onto cut museum board. Collection of the artist.

Five (Portrait of Lincoln) (2000), 6$\frac{1}{8}$" x 2$\frac{5}{8}$" collage of U.S. currency cut and pasted onto cut museum board. Collection of the artist.

Flag (1999), 2$\frac{3}{8}$" x 1$\frac{5}{8}$" collage on hand-cut museum board. Collection of the artist.

Frosted Flakes #1 (Portrait of an American Classic) (1996), 8$\frac{1}{2}$" x 11" cereal box collage on the cardboard from a writing pad. Private collection: St. Louis, Missouri.

The Gettysburg Address (2003), 20" x 30" collage composition on acid-free cardboard. Collection of the artist.

Judgement Day (2000), 32" x 40" collage composition on 8-ply black museum board. Collection of the artist.

The Last Breakfast (2001), 20" x 15" collage composition on white museum board. Collection of the artist.

Mount Rushmore (2004), 10" x 6" collage composition on hand-cut white museum board. Collection of the artist.

New York City (e)scape (1987), 9" x 5$\frac{7}{8}$" pen and marker on air sickness bag. Collection of the artist.

The Number Pi (The First 190 Digits) (2005), 10" x 10" collage composition on hand-cut white museum board. Collection of the artist.

The Pain of the Weight of the World (1992), 11$\frac{3}{4}$" x 11$\frac{3}{4}$" wax oil drawing on cardboard. Collection of the artist.

The Pledge of Allegiance (2004), 15" x 20" collage composition on white museum board. Collection of the artist.

The Signing of the Declaration of Independence (2005), 32" x 40" collage composition on 8-ply white museum board. Collection of the artist.

Sir Real Lemon Man (1995), 4$\frac{1}{4}$" x 4$\frac{5}{8}$" wax oil drawing on hand-cut illustration board. Collection of the artist.

Sir Real Red Apple Man (1994), 2" x 2" wax oil drawing on hand-cut museum board. Collection of the artist.

Sir Real Tangerine Man (1999), 2$\frac{1}{8}$" x 2$\frac{1}{2}$" collage of cereal boxes and photograph on hand-cut illustration board. Collection of the artist.

The Statue of Liberty ("The New Colossus") (2004), 15" x 20" collage composition on white museum board. Collection of the artist.

Trix (Master Cerealist Portrait) (1998), 15" x 20" collage composition of cereal boxes on museum board. Collection of the artist.

The Victim (1988), 28" x 22" wax oil drawing on oak tag. Private collection.

You Know What They Say (2003), 30" x 20" collage composition on white museum board. Collection of the artist.

PHOTO CREDITS

Newark (New Jersey) Museum of Art (summer youth arts program, July 1998), two photos (group shot and at work surrounded by students).

Parrish Art Museum (Make Something from Nothing Family Festival, Southampton, New York, September 1997), at work at the communal collage table.